Whispers and Footsteps

Also by Merili Freear

*Just Run: Discovering my love for running
and how the impossible becomes possible*

Whispers and Footsteps

Merili Freear

Copyright © Merili Freear, 2025

All rights reserved. No part of this publication may be reproduced, stored in a retrieval system, transmitted, or circulated in any form or by any means—electronic, mechanical, photocopying, recording, or otherwise—without prior written permission from the author.

For permissions, contact: meriliruns@gmail.com

A CIP catalogue record for this book is available from the British Library.

ISBN: Paperback: 978-1-7385559-2-5
ISBN: eBook: 978-1-7385559-4-9

Cover and interior design by the author.

To my husband, Paul.

You've been my calm, my courage, and my home.

Contents

Doubt 1
Darkness 15
Strength 31
Acceptance 47
Love 61
Becoming 71
Author's Note 83
About the Author.................................... 85

Doubt

The smallest whisper of 'maybe I can' is louder than 'what if I can't'.

I have spent too much time questioning myself—wondering if I am enough, if I am capable, if I truly deserve the things I've worked for.

Doubt has a way of whispering in your ear, making you believe you are smaller than you are.

These poems explore that voice, my inner gremlins—the one that tells us we aren't good enough—and the quiet fight to rise above it.

First

I don't want to post anything.
I just want to be.
I just want to be myself,
not what's expected of me.

I am not for them;
I am for me.
I am not perfect,
but I do my best to be authentic.

That's all I can do.
For me, I am enough.

What if?

What if I can't run a marathon a month?
What if I can't write another book?
What if I fail as a coach?
What if I'm a bad mother?

What if, what if, what if—
what if I can't?

...What if I can?

Fear of failure

avoid, avoid, avoid—
you might do great.
but what if you don't?
what if everything crumbles,
and you end up back where you started?

avoid, avoid, avoid—
what would the neighbours whisper?
what would the school parents see?

avoid, avoid, avoid—
but what if you let go?
what if you let yourself
be your best, wildest self?
what if you dared to try,
and found new wings to fly?

what if you succeed?

Out of reach

My goals seem so close,
yet always just beyond my grasp.

Is it luck you need,
or sheer determination?
Do you push through the doubt,
and hope for the best?

Surely, there must be more
you can do.

You try.
You hope.
You wait.

And one day, it will happen.

Relief

When I accomplish something,
I feel relief.

I should feel proud.
But I feel relief.

Relief that it's done.
Relief that I didn't fail.

Then—onto the next thing.
And the next.

Will it ever end?
Will I ever feel proud?

Depression doesn't define me

I am more than that.
I am brave.
I am resilient.
I am present.

Everyone else sees it—
why can't I?

Imposter

I am afraid they'll find out
who I really am.

I work so hard.
I have to.

Everyone is better than me.
What if they see through me?

Maybe I was just lucky.
If I could do it,
then anyone could.

I'm not really the person they think I am.

My heart pounds in my chest.
Am I a fraud?

But if this were a study,
it wouldn't be published—
the evidence isn't there.

I am not a fraud.
I am as great as they say.

I work hard,
and one day, I will believe it.

One day.

Do you know the feeling when something is ending?

You worked so hard,
proved you could do the impossible,
and then—it's done.
Gone.
Nothing left to chase.

Emptiness creeps in,
until the next goal calls your name.

What do you do?

I have so many roles—
they run through my head.

I am a mother.
A wife.
An aunt.
A poet.
An ultrarunner.
A running coach.
A homemaker.
A marketer.
A lifelong learner.
A dog mum.
A writer.

So why does my heart sink?
Why do I feel small?
Invisible.
Like I don't belong.

Do I need to belong?
Or am I just hanging out in the wrong places?

There are people who see me,
who call me one of them.

Here, I belong.
And it's lovely to be here.

Worry

Worry.
Worry.
Worry.

I am a worrier.
(I don't like uncertainty.)

I crave control—
but I am not a warrior.

Or am I?
Aren't worriers
just warriors in disguise?

Are you?

Darkness

Darkness doesn't always announce itself. Sometimes, it settles in slowly, unnoticed—soft as breath, heavy as stone.

There have been days I've struggled to feel joy, even when surrounded by beauty. I feared the night when running my first 100-miler—feared being alone with my thoughts. But it was also in the darkness that I discovered unexpected peace, companionship, and a strength I didn't know I had.

These poems live in that space—between fear and solace, doubt and resilience. They are a reaching out for light, even when we don't yet believe it's there.

A drunken poem

I don't like wine,
but I have it anyway.
It's a great escape,
from thoughts going
a hundred miles an hour—
even if it's just for a bit.

I don't like alcohol.
I don't like hangovers.
But I sip,
and I self-medicate.

Alive

climbing out of the window
into the soft white snow—
it's cold.
we shouldn't do this,
but we could.

we are alive.
we are cold, we are feeling.
soft snow turns crunchy
underfoot.

it's only for a moment.
depression doesn't define us.
we are alive.
we are alive.

back inside,
away from snow,
back to darkness.

It's the right thing to do

I open my eyes, and all I want to do
is sink deep into the bed,
pull the blanket over my head,
and just be.
Maybe in another lifetime.

Some days, I think, what if I were in an accident—
nothing serious,
but enough to rest in a hospital
on crispy white sheets.
(Are they really white, or am I daydreaming?)

Instead, I get up,
skip the yoga mat,
do my pilates routine—
quiet.
Everyone's still asleep.

Then, I head out with Jack, my dog,
prepare breakfast and lunches,
take my son to school,
run,
then coffee—
my first cup,
from the machine, not instant.

Now I have a chance to feel, to think.
I carry on.
It's the right thing to do.

I am doing great

Things are working out,
I can accomplish all I would like.
Work hard, then comes love—
love for work, not for life.

I write those things daily
to convince myself
that things are good,
even if they're not.

Fake it, until you make it.
Fake smiles, fake tan—
but it's not me.

Fake, fake, fake—
you'll believe it then.
Will I?

The science says
it will work out.

Grounded

I don't want to let everyone down
I just want to go home,
to lay on a soft rug
and lick my wounds.

I want to feel grounded,
my body sinking into the earth's embrace.
I breathe,
I release.

I feel better.
I feel in peace.
Good night.

I run

I have watched serial killers on my screen
for months.
There's comfort in the predictable—
in knowing what comes next.

It gets me thinking:
how our lives shape us.
Some of us become murderers,
while others don't.
We fight our demons in different ways.

I run through the woods,
I run on the road,
I run along grassy banks.
I run, and I run.

I run long,
until my demons disappear.

I am fine

I am fine.
I am walking on thin streets.

'Hi, I'm good. How are you?'

Swallowing my tears,
I keep going,
no matter how it feels.

You can do it.
And you will.

I am fine.
I am fine.

I am crashing into bed
after doomscrolling for hours.

Can't you see?
I am fine.

I am tired

I am in a place
of not feeling good again.
I am tired of feeling like this,
so, so tired.

I am tired of living my life like this,
never feeling truly happy.
I want to be happy.
I really want to be happy.

But I can't seem to feel it.
I need a change.
I will change.
I will be happy.

I am on holiday

Sad.
Depressed.
Not happy.

I need to be happy.
I need to be happy.

There's so much to be grateful for.
Why am I not happy?

I try.
I know I should.
I love the surroundings.
I like the scenery.

A beautiful seaside,
lovely trails—

why is it still so hard?
Why am I not happy?

If I try harder,
will I get there?

Trust

I find it difficult to trust life.
Constantly searching for answers—
horoscopes, tarot, you name it.

But the future is not set in stone.
We create our own path.
We are responsible for our own life.

Trust life.
Trust yourself.
You got this.

The weight I carried

I carried the weight of the world
on my shoulders,
the heaviness of my own mind.

I smiled. I pretended.
No one knew.

Until I stopped.
Until I let it go.

I am not hiding.
I am free.

Healing

Healing can only start
when you are ready.
When you are really ready.

A bandage doesn't heal the wound—
it just covers it.

To heal,
I need to hit rock bottom.
I need to feel the fight
burn inside me.

This demon—
it doesn't own me.
Depression doesn't own me.

I am in control.
I can heal.

If you don't rest

If you don't rest,
your body will decide for you—
it will force you when you least expect it.

I am done with depression.
I am done with burnout.

I don't see a way out yet—
but I will.
I will.

Strength

Even when your voice shakes, your footsteps still count.

It's about resilience, endurance, and the quiet determination to keep going. It's in the moments we refuse to give up, the times we push through doubt, and the times we allow ourselves to rest so we can rise again.

These poems are about finding power in movement, in persistence, and in the belief that we are stronger than we know.

It will happen

It will happen
when you accept,
when you let go.

It will happen
when you stop searching.
It's there—
suddenly,
it's there.

It happened.

Always trust:
good things happen to
good people.
Believe.

I can do hard things

I say this to myself often,
and some days, I believe me.
I know I can do hard things,
though my inner gremlins disagree.

'Are you sure?' they whisper.
But I put my foot down and answer:
'I can do hard things.'

Why I run?

I don't run to win races,
I don't run to compete.
I run to heal my spirit,
I run to find my peace.

I run to quiet chaos,
I run to feel alive.
Step by step, I rediscover
The strength to truly thrive.

Whispers and footsteps

I want to go home,
I want to go home.
But I don't.
I surrender and carry on,
closer to the darkness.

The forest is quiet;
the forest is dark.
Yet I am at peace—
I know what is to come.

I silence my whispering gremlins,
focus on my footsteps
against the soft forest floor.
I keep running,
until—

a rustle, a rhythm,
the footsteps of a newfound friend.
I know I won't be alone.

The forest holds me,
quiet and dark.
I am not alone.

I ran today

I missed the sound of my footsteps—
on trails, on roads,
one with my thoughts,
fully present.

Focusing on what I can do,
not what I have to do.

Dreaming.
Believing.
Anything is possible.

Control

I read a study:
communities without control
were more prone to suicide.

I want to control everything.

But we can only control
our thoughts,
our actions.

What makes us miserable
is trying to control
the uncontrollable.

God, grant me the serenity
to accept the things I cannot change,
courage to change the things I can,
and wisdom
to know the difference.

I used to think

I used to think strength meant never falling.
I know better now.

Strength is getting up,
again and again.
Not for others—
but for myself.

Trying, failing,
and trying again.

I am worth the effort.
I am worth the love.

I stand tall,
like a mighty oak.

I am the oak.

We all make mistakes

We all make mistakes.
Some small.
Some that keep us awake at night.

Only those who do nothing
make none.

I will fail.
I will stumble.
I will get it wrong.

But I will also learn.
I will also grow.
And I will try again.

You got this

These are the words I say to myself, often—
you got this.

You don't have to have all the answers.
You don't have to know what the future holds.
You just have to keep going.

You got this.

Not because they say so.
Not because you have to.
But because you do.
Because you always have.

The version of me I haven't met yet

I find it hard to let go,
to trust that I will be okay.

But every experience shapes me.
I have fallen before—
and I have gotten up.

So I know,
whatever happens,
I can do it again.

And so will you.

I am amazing

This is how I feel today:
my accomplishments are worthy.
I am beautiful.
I am smart.
I am a great writer,
a great friend,
mum, and wife.

Today, I believe it.
Hopefully, tomorrow
won't change my mind.

You are enough.

Acceptance

Let go of who you were. Celebrate who you are.

For so long, I focused on everything I wasn't. I saw my flaws before I saw my strengths. Learning to love myself—my body, my mind, all of me—has been one of the hardest things I've ever done. Gratitude and self-love don't always come naturally, but they are choices we can make every day.

These poems are reminders to be kind to ourselves, to appreciate the bodies that carry us, and to celebrate how far we've come.

Let the past go

Leave it behind—
it doesn't define you.

It has shaped you
into the person you are today,
but you don't have to carry its burden.

Look forward.
The past is behind you.

I see a new day,
a new start.
What do you see?

It's the only body I've got

I love it.
I love my imperfect legs,
my imperfect arms.

Instead of cellulite,
I focus not on how I look
but on what this body can do.

It carried me 100 miles in one go.
It carried my son to term.
It's always been with me,
despite all I've put it through—
steadfast, patient, and true.

I think it likes me.
And I like it too.

Quiet

I need quiet.
My mind is busy all the time.
I don't want TV.
I don't want music.
I don't even want to hear my thoughts.

I just want quiet—
no dogs barking,

no kids playing,
the beautiful sound of nothing.

I am safe

I am free
from the demons of my past.
They can't reach me anymore.

I am here,
I have moved on.
They have no hold.
I control my life.

All I have is love—
love for myself,
love for my family.

My demons,
they'll never return.

Learning to be proud

It's not easy to be proud.
I try my best.

'Well done. You are amazing.'
Lioness.

You are.
Be proud.

I try my best.
Maybe one day it gets easier,
to be proud of myself.

And I believe it.
Everyone else believes in me.
One day, I will too.

Tomorrow

That magical tomorrow.

Tomorrow, I'll start a diet.
Tomorrow, I'll eat better.
Tomorrow, I'll exercise again.

Tomorrow.
But what about today?
What about now?

You are alive right now.
Start today.
Start now.

Joy in surrender

We can't control the uncontrollable.
I drive myself mad trying to hold
everything.

When I lose control of some things,
I grip tighter to others.
It's not healthy.
I know that now.

Maybe strength is loosening the grip.
Maybe peace is found in release.

Control.
Losing control.
Letting go.

Surrender.
There's joy in surrender.
Joy.

I need to write

Writing keeps me sane.
I can process my thoughts,
ideas,
dreams—
all on paper.

Anything is possible.
Pigs can fly,
and I could be happy.

You believe me,
don't you?

I am reading again

I love books.
When I am lost,
I search for myself
in other people's words.

When I am ready,
I connect—
to the cream pages,
to the scent of ink and paper,
to the quiet escape between the lines.

I love how books make me feel—
connected,
present,
alive.

Disconnecting

We do so much to be seen,
to have an online presence,
that we forget—

the only thing
that truly heals us
is putting the phone away,
closing social media.

That's it.

Love

Love doesn't always arrive the way we imagined. It just feels like coming home.

Love isn't just romance. It's the way we show up for the people in our lives, the way we find connection in unexpected places, the way we learn to be there for ourselves. Some of us spend years searching for love, only to realise it was around us all along.

These poems explore the meaning of love—not just the love we give to others, but the love we learn to give ourselves.

Family ties

The need to be accepted by your birth family,
to be someone they can be proud of.

But sometimes, closeness isn't found in shared DNA.
We can choose our own people.

Often, the people closest to us
are not tied to us by blood.
They might be friends,
neighbours,
the ones who stay.

Who would you want by your side
when you leave this world?

Loving myself in pieces

I chose to treat myself to the best chocolate,
even when I didn't think I deserved it.

I told myself, *it's okay*
when I made mistakes.
We all make mistakes.
It's okay—as long as we learn.

I forgave the reflection in the mirror.
It's my body,
and it deserves love,
no matter the clothes size.

Loving myself
wasn't a single moment.
It was many little moments—
small kindnesses,
treating myself like a friend.

I loved myself in pieces,
until one day,
I saw the whole me—

perfect,
imperfect.

Yes, that's me.

If I could see myself

If I could see myself
as others see me,
what would I see?
A lioness,
a quiet lady,
resilient,
amazing,
an inspiration.

Why can't I see myself
through their eyes?

It's hard to love me

It's hard to love me.
All I see is imperfection.

I look into the mirror.
I am here.
Today.

Perfectly imperfect.
Worthy of love.

My love.

Love is in the little things

Love is—
in my Sunday morning coffee,
in a warm meal I didn't have to cook,
in laundry folded for me,
in fresh flowers on the table after a long trip.

Love is—
in a simple touch when passing by,
in quiet moments of me-time when I need it most.

Love is in the little things.

I am grateful

Ten things, every day,
I write them down—
ten things.

I am grateful for my family,
grateful for the time to care for myself,
grateful for the good things coming my way,
grateful to be alive.

Ten things,
every day,
I am grateful.

Love

I am loving myself more every day.
I am worth it.
I love my floppy thighs
and imperfect arms,
my double chin
and my new grey hair.

These things make me *me*.
I don't need to change,
I don't need to fit a mould.

I am more than enough, just as I am.
Each flaw is a story,
each imperfection a reminder
that I have lived,
that I am human.

Becoming

Becoming isn't changing into someone new. It's returning to who you've always been.

Healing isn't a straight path. Some days, I feel like I've figured it out. Other days, I feel like I'm starting over. But what I do know is that I am moving forward. I am learning, I am growing, and I am becoming the person I was always meant to be.

These final poems are about hope, about believing in the future, and about trusting that one day, things will feel lighter.

So many versions of her

So many versions of her,
trying to fit the mould,
doing what's expected,
living someone else's life.

It doesn't work.

I need to find her.
Free her.
Accept her.

She is me.

One day, when I grow up

I wake up and realise—
I am the person
I once dreamed of becoming.

As a child, I said,
'One day, when I grow up',
I will do all the things.
I scribbled in notebooks,
whispered in quiet daydreams.

One day, when I grow up.
I wake up—
and realise,
I did.

The day has come.
I am the person
I wanted to become.

The weight of my name

I almost left my poetry unnamed.
I was scared—
scared of what others would say,
of what they would think
when I let myself be vulnerable,
when I let myself be *me*.

But they don't matter.

What matters is what I feel.
My voice.
My truth.

No empty words.
Just truth.

A letter to my future self

Dear me,

You will try, and you will fail.
You will try again.
And again.

The main thing? You will be okay.

You will love yourself the way others do—
fully, without conditions.

You will have found the things that truly matter.
The little joys:
the sun warming your nose,
the rich aroma of Sunday morning coffee,
the hush of early morning trails.

Whatever happens, you will be okay.

After a perfect morning

After a perfect morning,
the weight of my own thoughts
settles heavy on my shoulders.

I search for what I did wrong,
why I feel this way—
that familiar ache creeping in.

Why has *I can* turned into *I can't* again?

I remind myself—
I don't have to have it all figured out,
not all the time.

So I sit.
I rest.
I sip my coffee.

And I know—this will pass.

On days my heart feels heavy

On days when my heart feels heavy,
and my thoughts pull me under,
growth still happens.

Even a diamond is shaped by pressure
before it shines.

My future successes are built
beneath the weight of this moment,
underneath the fog,
beneath the doubt.

I am growing—
stronger,
resilient,
brave.

My life-house

I am building myself back up

brick by brick.
It's not instant,
it takes time.

Some walls fall,
only to be built again.
Some stay solid.

My life-house
will never be fully finished—
and that's okay.

Some years,
the fruit trees in my garden
overflow with sweetness.
Other years,
the cold takes them all.

But still,
I love my house.
I love my garden.
I love me.

The moment I knew I was okay

I had been walking in a fog for months,
not knowing if I was going the right way,
not seeing clearly where I was headed.

I was lost—
lost in my thoughts,
lost in my life.

Then suddenly, I stopped.
I couldn't get out of bed.
My sheets were too soft,
my pillow too inviting.

As I lay there,
listening to the quiet outside,
I recognised the silence.
The same one I remembered from childhood—
the sound of 1-3 nap time.

And in that moment,
I knew I would be okay.

There was no fog.
I wasn't lost.

I was just tired.

I slept for what felt like a thousand years,
and when I woke up,
I was okay.

Author's Note

If you've made it to the last page, thank you for being here with me.

These poems were written in moments of doubt, darkness, strength, and healing. If you saw yourself in these words, I hope they reminded you that you are not alone.

Healing isn't linear. Growth isn't instant. We are all building ourselves up—brick by brick, breath by breath.

There is something I would like you to remember every day—you are enough.

About the Author

Merili Freear is a poet, ultrarunner, and the author of *Just Run*. Her writing explores themes of self-love, healing, resilience, and identity—with a voice that is both gentle and unflinchingly honest.

Through her poetry and storytelling, she quietly encourages others to reflect, reset, and reconnect with themselves, finding joy in the small things, and reminding us all that we are already enough.

She lives in the UK with her husband, son, and their dog, where she continues to chase sunrises, words, and the quiet magic of becoming.

You can connect with her on social media:
Instagram: @whispersandfootsteps
TikTok: @whispersandfootsteps

A Small Favour

Thank you for taking the time to read my words. If these poems touched you in any way, I'd be deeply grateful if you'd consider leaving a review.

Reviews help more than you know. They help others discover this book, and maybe find a little of themselves in its pages too.

You can leave a review on Amazon, Goodreads, or wherever you purchased or discovered this book. Every kind word truly makes a difference.

www.ingramcontent.com/pod-product-compliance
Lightning Source LLC
Chambersburg PA
CBHW020544080526
44583CB00013B/994